THE
ARAPAHO INDIANS

THE JUNIOR LIBRARY OF
AMERICAN INDIANS

THE
ARAPAHO INDIANS

Vicki Haluska

CHELSEA HOUSE PUBLISHERS
New York   Philadelphia

FRONTISPIECE: Northern Arapaho chief Black Coal, photographed in 1882

CHAPTER TITLE ORNAMENT: A symbol used in Arapaho beadwork to represent a tipi

Chelsea House Publishers
EDITOR-IN-CHIEF Richard S. Papale
MANAGING EDITOR Karyn Gullen Browne
COPY CHIEF Philip Koslow
PICTURE EDITOR Adrian G. Allen
ART DIRECTOR Nora Wertz
MANUFACTURING DIRECTOR Gerald Levine
SYSTEMS MANAGER Lindsey Ottman
PRODUCTION COORDINATOR Marie Claire Cebrián-Ume

The Junior Library of American Indians
SENIOR EDITOR Liz Sonneborn

Staff for THE ARAPAHO INDIANS
ASSOCIATE EDITOR Martin Schwabacher
COPY EDITOR Danielle Janusz
EDITORIAL ASSISTANT Nicole Greenblatt
DESIGNER Debora Smith
PICTURE RESEARCHER Sandy Jones
COVER ILLUSTRATOR Vilma Ortiz

3 5 7 9 8 6 4

Library of Congress Cataloging-in-Publication Data

Haluska, Vicki.
The Arapaho Indians/Vicki Haluska
    p. cm.—(The Junior Library of American Indians)
Includes index.
Summary: Examines the life and culture of the Arapaho Indians.
        ISBN 0-7910-1657-9
        ISBN 0-7910-1960-8 (pbk.)
1. Arapaho Indians—Juvenile literature. [1. Arapaho Indians.
2. Indians of North America.] I. Title. II. Series.
E99.A7H35 1993   92-18743
973'.04973—dc20   CIP
                                                  AC

CONTENTS

CHAPTER **1**

Creation

In the beginning of time, there was no earth—only water. Floating on its surface, on a seat made of four sticks, was the Father, also known as the Keeper of the Flat Pipe.

One day, the Father called to the waterfowl that swam around him. He asked the birds to dive into the water and search for the bottom of the sea. When they found the bottom, they were to scoop up some dirt with their feet and bring it back to him.

One by one, the waterfowl dove in. First, the largest bird plunged into the water. Then the next largest bird dove and was followed by still the next largest. The divers' bodies soon rose to the surface. All had drowned.

Finally it was the duck's turn to dive. The duck was timid and not so sure it could reach the bottom, but it wanted to try. The duck dove into the depths and remained there for several days and nights. The Father waited close by, hoping the duck would emerge alive.

Suddenly the water began to move, and the duck burst through the surface. The Father grabbed it and cleaned the mud from its feet. He carefully placed the mud on the Flat Pipe and sadly realized that he still needed more dirt.

Just then, the turtle swam toward the Father. The turtle said that it too would like to try its luck and dove into the sea. After many days and nights, bubbles began to rise to the surface, signaling the animal's return. When the turtle emerged, the Father found that its feet were stuck together. He pulled them apart and discovered there was mud on all four feet.

The Father added this clay to that brought up by the duck and spread it all out in a thin layer. When it was dry, he took a pinch of dirt and blew it to the Northeast, the Southeast, the Northwest, and the Southwest. The Father then flung the rest of the dirt out in a circle. He declared that this would form the Earth. With a special rod, the Father made

In this 1908 photograph by Edward Curtis, a woman carries her child on a travois, a set of poles dragged behind a horse or dog.

motions over the water to create rivers. In places where the dirt was thick, he used the rod to make mountains.

After creating the Sun and the Moon, the Father said, "I have to have servants to watch over the Earth." From clay, he molded a man and a woman and then gave them the gift of life. He also created all plants and animals and the cycle of the seasons.

This is the story of creation as told by a Southern Arapaho Indian almost 100 years

ago. Stories such as this have been handed down by the Arapahos for generations. Grandparents and other elders use these stories to pass Arapaho values and beliefs on to Arapaho children. In this way, youngsters learn how to behave and how to earn respect among their people. The history of the tribe is also conveyed through these tales.

The Arapaho people have lived in the Great Plains of what is now the central United States for hundreds of years. Instead of staying in one place, they followed the great herds of buffalo that roamed free. By hunting the buffalo, they obtained food, materials to make clothing and shelter, and almost everything else they needed.

In the 1700s, they came in contact with non-Indians. The Arapahos were curious about these strangers. They were especially interested in the goods the newcomers brought to trade. Quickly, the tribe became known as wise traders among both whites and Indians. The name Arapaho may come from the Pawnee Indian word *tirapihu*, which means "trader."

Another possible source of their name is the Crow Indian word *alappahó*, meaning "people with many tattoos." Arapaho men typically had three small circles tattooed across their chests, and women had a single

THE DIVISION OF THE ARAPAHOS IN THE MID-1800s

CANADA

NORTH DAKOTA

Arikaras
Hidatsas

MINNESOTA

WISCONSIN

MONTANA

Crows

Northern Cheyennes

SOUTH DAKOTA

Mississippi River

WYOMING

R o c k y

Missouri River

IOWA

Sioux

North Platte River

NEBRASKA

Shoshones

M o u n t a i n s

Platte River

Northern Arapahos

Utes

UTAH

South Platte River

Denver

KANSAS

St. Louis

MISSOURI

Southern Arapahos

Arkansas River

COLORADO

Southern Cheyennes

ARKANSAS

North Canadian River

Santa Fe

Canadian River

NEW MEXICO

OKLAHOMA

CANADA

area of map

UNITED STATES

MEXICO

Comanches

TEXAS

N

W   E

S

LOUISIANA

(modern state and international boundaries)

circle tattooed on their foreheads. The tattoos were made by pricking the skin with
cactus spines and rubbing powdered charcoal into the wounds, which became sky
blue when they healed.

In the 1850s, white settlers and gold miners began to flock to the Arapahos' hunting
grounds. Unlike the traders who came before
them, these people did not want to give
the Arapahos anything. They wanted to take
something away—land. The Arapahos' favorite campsite along the headwaters of the
South Platte River in what is now Colorado
was taken over by non-Indian settlers. Denver and other towns sprang up, disturbing the
grazing routes of the buffalo.

Eventually, the Arapahos permanently split
into two groups. The miners and homesteaders drove the Northern Arapahos farther north to Wyoming, while the Southern
Arapahos stayed south of the crowded Denver area. Both groups of Arapahos were unhappy and angry at being separated from
their relatives. But they remained one people
with one language.

As more and more whites moved west, the
Arapahos' problems grew. The newcomers'
government took control of more land and
told the Indians they had to make do with
less. In time, it forced the Arapahos to settle

on small tracts of land called *reservations*. Unable to travel through the plains, it became impossible for them to live as they had in the past. These were hard and painful times for the tribe.

But despite their many difficulties, the Arapahos have survived. Today, there are still two divisions of the tribe. The Northern Arapahos continue to live on the Wind River Reservation in Wyoming. The Southern Arapahos have no reservation, and most now live in small towns in west-central Oklahoma.

Each year, members of both groups come together in Wyoming. In a ceremony, they renew their ties to one another and to the past through prayers and fasting. They also act out the story of the Father and how, with the help of the duck and the turtle, he created the world. The story reminds them that even though much time has passed they are still the Father's creations. They are still the Arapahos. ▲

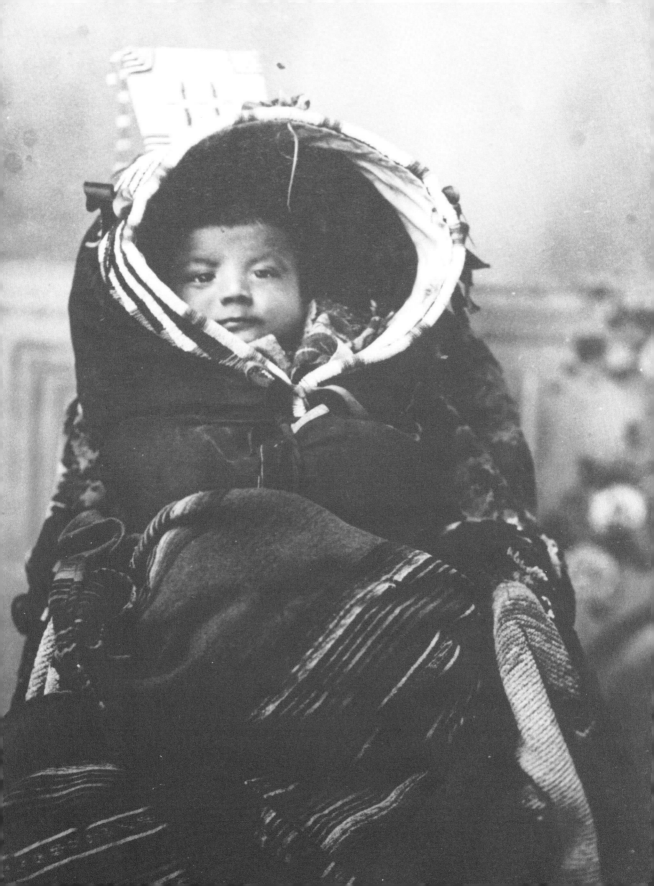

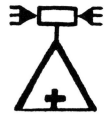

A Southern Arapaho baby in a cloth cradle. Cradles were traditionally made of leather, but by the late 1800s there were no longer enough animals to supply the Arapahos with skins.

CHAPTER **2**

The Four Hills of Life

The Arapahos viewed life as a cycle, like that of the seasons. Between birth and death, an Arapaho passed through four stages or "hills of life"—childhood, youth, adulthood, and old age. After death, a person could be born again. Wrinkles on a baby might mean that an elder had been reborn, while scars were thought to be wounds from a previous life.

When a baby was born, it was painted with red earth to bring strength and good health. Elders prayed for the baby. Their prayers were especially valued because their long life was seen as a blessing from the Creator.

A Southern Arapaho child. When a child first learned to walk, parents invited tribal elders to a special feast.

Soon after birth, the child was named by an elder. Elders might name the baby after a brave deed they had done, or something seen in a dream or vision. When an elder gave the child his or her own name, it was believed to bring a long, healthy life. If the child became ill, however, the name was often changed.

When the child first walked or spoke, elders were invited to a special feast. Other important events, such as when a boy killed his first animal, were also marked by feasts and prayers.

As they grew up, children learned about adult tasks through their play. Girls played with toy tipis that were two to three feet tall and contained beds made of squirrel skins. Little boys played war games, using horses and men made of clay. Children were given ponies and began to ride when they were only three years old. Later, the boys' games included shooting arrows, throwing javelins, and spinning tops. Girls played with balls and dice.

Children began their training for adult life at around age 12. Boys and girls were separated from one another—even brothers and sisters. After puberty, a girl would often go to live with her grandmother or another female elder. There she was taught to prepare food, tan hides, and make clothing. She also learned to perfume her hair and clothes with sweet-smelling leaves and seeds.

Teenage boys began their training by participating in the Kit Fox ceremony. A group of boys would ask a man about 10 years older to be their adviser. He taught them songs and dances for the ceremony. As Kit Foxes they trained together, racing on foot and horseback, wrestling, and fighting mock battles. The boys also promised to assist and support each other for the rest of their lives.

Young men in their late teens continued their training with the Star Ceremony, becoming Starmen. Both ceremonies were preparation for the sacred societies or *lodges* a man could join throughout his life. Joining a lodge was thought to bring supernatural power. Men who did not join the lodges could never earn responsible positions or respect in the community.

The Tomahawk Lodge was the first of four major lodges joined by men at approximately 10-year intervals. To join the Tomahawk Lodge, each Starman found an older man to advise him and performed a seven-day ritual believed to give him great power and strength. Later, the Spear Lodge provided supernatural aid against danger or ill health. As members of the Crazy Lodge, men learned of secret plants that could paralyze enemies or animals. They also learned to walk on hot coals. At about age 50, men could join the Dog Lodge. Dogmen directed battles and became tribal leaders.

Men of any age could participate in the *Offerings* or *Sacrifice Lodge*, also known as the *Sun Dance*. An important part of the Sun Dance ritual was self-torture, which could include cutting off pieces of flesh. Men would go without food or water and dance day and night until they had hallucinatory visions, which were believed to be messages from the Creator. The Offerings Lodge was the most respected because it called for great physical suffering and large donations of property by those participating. The Offerings Lodge was considered vital to the physical and spiritual well-being of all Arapahos.

Before they could marry, men had to prove their skill in hunting, fighting, and raiding other tribes for their horses. By age 30, most were confident they could take care of a wife and family. Young women married in their late teens.

Marriages were arranged by a woman's male relative, usually an older brother. He

A young Arapaho woman, photographed by Edward Curtis in 1910.

would choose a man thought to be a good provider, often one of his friends. A man could ask to marry a particular woman he admired. A woman could refuse to marry a man if she did not like him, but she usually accepted her relatives' choice.

On the wedding day, the groom's family delivered presents, including horses, to the bride's family. In return, the bride's family gave an equal amount of property to the family of the groom. Following the exchange of gifts, the bride's family put up a *tipi* and furnished it. Because it was a wedding present to the woman from her family, it remained the wife's property. At the wedding feast, elders of the tribe prayed for the young couple and instructed them on how to enjoy a successful marriage.

An Arapaho man generally had a second wife. If he was very wealthy, he might have three or four wives. When a man married for the second time, the first, or "boss," wife directed all household work. Often a man would marry the younger sister of his first wife. This tradition ensured a strong friendship between his two wives. A man, his wives, their children, and perhaps a widowed parent or a younger brother of the husband might live together in one tipi.

Tipis were made in a cone shape from tall poles covered with 15 to 20 buffalo hides sewn together. The tipi was lined inside, and on this lining were painted pictures of the husband's brave deeds in battle.

A platform made of poles was used as a combination bed and couch. It stood one foot above the dirt floor and was covered by a woven mat of willow rods. On top of that were placed warm, soft animal hides and deerskin pillows stuffed with buffalo fur.

In the center of the tipi a fire was kept burning with wood or dried *buffalo chips* (droppings). The family ate whenever they were hungry, or when a hunter returned with meat. A common meal was a stew of meat, herbs, and wild roots such as turnips and potatoes, cooked in a rawhide pouch. The water was heated by dropping red-hot stones into it.

Like most Plains Indians, the Arapahos depended upon the buffalo for survival. They ate its meat; used its hide for tipis, robes, and blankets; made tools, including knives and spoons, from its bones; and burned its droppings for fuel. Ground buffalo chips were even packed around a baby in its cradle to keep it dry.

Before horses were introduced to the Americas by the Spaniards in the 1500s, the Arapahos hunted buffalo on foot. They learned how to drive a few out of the main herd and chase them over a cliff, and then finish them off with arrows. With horses, hunting became much easier. Arapaho men were excellent riders. While racing on horse-

An Arapaho camp, photographed in the early 1870s. The tipi is made of sewn buffalo skins. In the background, a fresh hide hangs on a rack to dry.

back alongside a buffalo, a skilled hunter could fell the animal with a single arrow.

In the spring, families gathered together for the buffalo hunt. Hundreds of tipis were arranged in a vast circle for the summer. The center of the camp was used for ceremonies and lodge initiations, most lasting several days. Those men not participating in a ceremony went off in groups to hunt or perhaps to steal horses from enemy tribes.

Women did a variety of chores around the camp, such as gathering wild herbs and berries, and making pemmican. Pemmican consisted of buffalo meat and wild berries blended with fat and left to dry in the summer air. During the winter months it was a staple food for Indian families.

As winter returned, each band of 20 to 80 related families moved back to its chosen campsite in the sheltered forests along mountain streams. Men wore snowshoes as they hunted small game, and used bone whistles to lure deer.

Moving and setting up the tipi and all of its contents was a task done by women. Their other chores included carrying water, collecting firewood, and cooking for their families. They tanned hides, sewed tipi covers, and made all the clothing. Women also cured meat and gathered herbs and roots.

Despite all the hard work necessary for survival, Arapaho men and women devoted a great deal of time to the enrichment of their spiritual lives. Through prayer, both men and women could petition the Creator for supernatural power for their personal use.

A man might go to a mountaintop to fast and meditate for several days in hopes of being visited by a supernatural being. If the being came to him, it appeared first as an animal and then took a human form. The being might grant the power to cure sickness, succeed in war, control the weather, or tell the future. Both men and women might receive supernatural powers from beings that came to them in dreams. For example, a woman might be given instructions on how to use a particular herb for healing.

The various objects a man or woman might need to bring on his or her powers were carried in a small pouch called a "medicine bag." One could give or sell supernatural powers to another, along with the medicine bag and instructions for its use. Supernatural power was not taken lightly. Using it for evil purposes could bring harm to the bag's owner as well as the intended victim.

Old people were believed to have the most spiritual power. Men about 60 years old performed a very sacred ceremony called the

Stoic Lodge, which included four nights of fasting and prayer. Stoicmen were supposed to think only good thoughts, because their prayers were considered so powerful that whatever they wished for was thought to occur. The Stoic Lodge ceremony was considered so sacred that young people did not go near it.

All the sacred lodges were presided over by seven tribal priests called the "Water-Pouring Old Men." When the bands were

Tent of the keeper of the sacred pipe, used at a Northern Arapaho Sun Dance in 1900.

camped together in the summer, these men prayed daily in a large, domed "sweat lodge" in the center of the camp. They poured water over hot coals, creating steam. The upward movement of the steam was thought to carry their prayers to the Creator.

Religious rituals seeking the protection and aid of the Creator guided the Arapahos on their path through the four hills of life. This traditional way of life was challenged, however, when newcomers pushed westward onto their lands. ▲

The great herds of buffalo that once filled the Great Plains, as drawn by George Catlin around 1832.

CHAPTER 3

Outnumbered

In 1803 the United States bought a huge body of land from the French. Known as the Louisiana Purchase, it stretched from the Mississippi River to the Rocky Mountains and included the land on which the Arapahos lived. President Thomas Jefferson called for an expedition to explore the territory.

The explorers set out from St. Louis, Missouri, in May 1804, led by Meriwether Lewis and William Clark. Along their route they met with many Indian groups and wrote of them in their journals. When Americans read about the Indian way of life, the endless herds of buffalo roaming the prairie, and the majestic peaks of the Rocky Mountains, many set out to see these wonders for themselves.

Non-Indians became a common sight to the Plains Indians after the Lewis and Clark expedition. Many of the newcomers were trappers in search of beaver pelts. Some were seeking gold. The whites brought with them things the Indians had never seen or heard of. The Arapahos traded buffalo robes for novelties such as glass beads, woven cloth, metal knives and pots, and tobacco.

Before the whites arrived, the Arapahos had traded with other Indians. They acquired horses in the 1730s from tribes to the southwest, who had gotten them from the Spanish. Riding horses made travel easier, and the Arapahos began trading with distant tribes. They visited the farming villages of the Arikara, Mandan, and Hidatsa Indians on the Missouri River. The Arapahos gave meat and hides to the tribes in exchange for beans, corn, and squash.

The buffalo, however, was their main source of livelihood. Nearly every part of the animal was used for food, shelter, or clothing. At the time Lewis and Clark made their expedition, the buffalo population was estimated to be 60 million. Another explorer, John Charles Frémont, reported that in the 1820s and 1830s, buffalo herds were never out of a traveler's sight from the Missouri River to the Rocky Mountains.

A Northern Arapaho *"friendly chief" named Friday. As a child, Friday was reared for seven years by a white man before returning to his people.*

The buffalo's grazing patterns, however, were severely disrupted by non-Indian settlers. The United States was a young, growing country and encouraged its citizens to seek opportunities in the West. In the 1840s, the Oregon Trail became the main route for travelers moving to what are now the states of Utah, Oregon, and California. It followed the North Platte River through Arapaho land. The discovery of gold in California in 1848 brought so much traffic along the Oregon Trail that the buffalo disappeared, leaving many Indians without meat or hides for their tipis.

In 1848 the United States won a war with Mexico, gaining a vast amount of land in what is now Texas. The land was opened to homesteaders, who traveled through Arapaho territory by following the Santa Fe Trail along the Arkansas River.

With so many non-Indians traveling across their land and driving away the buffalo, the Arapahos faced a major problem. Some of the other Plains Indians attacked the whites as they trampled uninvited through Indian territory. But the Arapahos tried another approach.

Along both the Santa Fe Trail and the Oregon Trail, wagon trains saw long lines of Arapahos mounted on horseback. Waving

Continued on page 41

POWERFUL SYMBOLS

Before the Arapahos met non-Indians, they made everything they needed themselves. Men made objects that were used in war and for hunting, including shields, weapons, and tools. Women created all household items, from clothing to carrying bags to tipi covers.

The Arapahos decorated many of the things they made. For example, they might sew beads on a carrying pouch to make a colorful design. Or they might paint pictures of animals on a deerskin skirt or dress.

With paint, beads, and other ornaments, the Arapahos could made a treasured object beautiful. But the decorations on some items had an extra meaning. These designs were called *hiiteni*. They were thought to have a special power.

Arapaho artists sometimes saw hiiteni in dreams or in visions. They often also saw a spirit who told them to make a certain object and use the hiiteni to adorn it.

Some hiiteni were handed down from older artists to younger ones. Such gifts kept the hiiteni's power alive from generation to generation.

A beaded tipi ornament, Southern Arapaho. The concentric arcs represent the whirlwind that was present at the creation of the earth; the sawtooth pattern around the circumference represents human beings. Four narrow black-edged white sectors divide the circular ornament into four larger sectors. Together, the colors red, yellow, black, and white signify the four directions. Four such ornaments were attached around the tipi, with a fifth at the front top. The design and the ceremony in which it was made represent a prayer for a good life, a life in harmony with all of creation.

Girl's buckskin Ghost Dance dress, Southern Arapaho. The designs, seen in a devotee's dream, include the Thunderbird (at center bottom), the buffalo (symbolizing subsistence in the fresh, new world to come), the morning star (whose green edges denote the freshness of that world), and the magpie (a messenger to the spirit world). The black shapes are hiiteni. Other designs include a turtle (symbolic of creation), a cottonwood tree, stars and a new moon (the heavens), a rainbow surrounding a cloud, and a green strip (the rebirth of the earth in springtime). The netted hoop at center suggests a children's game revived in Ghost Dance times.

Ghost Dance feather headdress, Southern Arapaho. It signified the expected return of the dead because spirits seen in visions wore such headdresses.

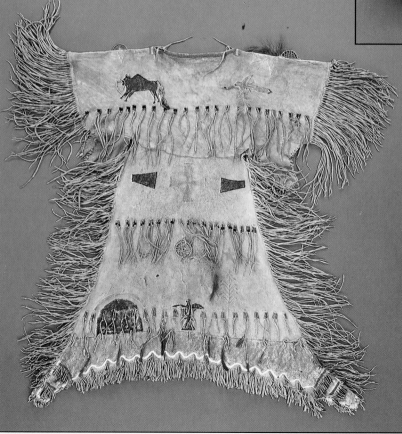

Head ornament worn at peyote ceremony, Southern Arapaho. The 12 feathers, which represent sticks in the ceremonial fire, are attached to knotted leather thongs. The metal knob represents the sacramental peyote button and the bead-covered handle the peyote plant. The blue feathers symbolize ashes from the ceremonial fire.

Painted sheet with designs seen in a dream, worn as a robe during the Ghost Dance, Southern Arapaho. The birds are an eagle (right, on the rainbow), a bull-bat bird (right) and magpie flying across the sky (background), and the crow messenger (left, on the rainbow), who took the dreamer to a cloud and related the coming of the new world. The wavy lines carry the birds' voices to the heavens. Also represented are the morning star (cross) and the earth (red in lower corners).

Cradle, Northern Arapaho. The round, quilled ornament symbolizes the baby's head as well as a tipi ornament. Other ornaments also represent parts of the child's body as well as parts of a tipi. Red is the child's blood, black his hair as a youth and adult, and white his hair in old age. In making this cradle the craftswoman created a prayer that the child would live long and inhabit his own tipi as he inhabited his cradle.

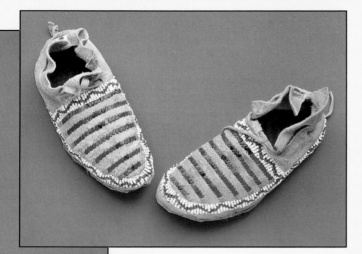

Child's moccasins, Northern Arapaho. The craftswoman symbolized her prayer that the child's path through life would be safe (avoiding snake bites—the green zigzag beading) and reach old age (to use the sweat house, whose poles and heated stones are represented by the multicolored quillwork).

Girl's leggings and moccasins, Southern Arapaho. The red quill rows are the girl's path through life; the blue beaded triangles are the designs on the rawhide bags she will make. Also shown are hiiteni and animal tracks. The tin rattles frighten snakes.

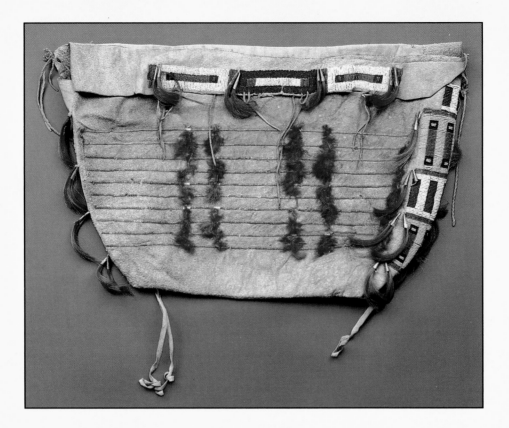

Large, soft hide bag, Southern Arapaho. The quilled stripes represent marks made by tipi poles being dragged when the camp moves. The wool tuft stripes are ravines where camp is set up; the beaded rectangles are hiiteni; the feathers are drying buffalo meat. The bag is a prayer for prosperity.

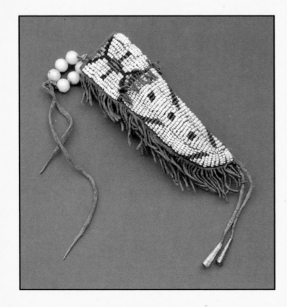

Woman's beaded knife case, Northern Arapaho. The cross at the top represents a person; the triangles above and below it are mountains. The squares below are hiiteni; the wedges that point to them are prayers for desired goals.

Woman's pouch for combs and body paint, Northern Arapaho. The entire beaded design is a wish for prosperity and a good life. Designs represent morning stars (the center crosses), bear claws (the three-pronged shapes), tipis (the pink triangles) separated by trails, and mountain ranges (the border). The designs on the sides at the top are meat-drying racks. On the flap are mountains (triangles) and lakes (squares).

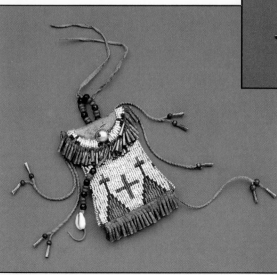

Woman's belt pouch for small items, Northern Arapaho. The overall design is a prayer for prosperity. Symbols include the morning star (the center cross), eagles on tipi poles (crosses on triangles), and meat-drying racks (on the flap).

Parfleche for porcupine quills, Northern Arapaho. The diamond rows represent strings of silver disks worn by prosperous men. Also symbolic of abundance are the colors, which stand for all green, yellow, and red objects, and the unpainted triangles, which are tents.

Parfleche, painted rawhide, Northern Arapaho. The entire design symbolizes the earth and is a prayer for a prosperous, satisfying life. The blue shapes are mountains in whose centers are unpainted valleys, red hills, and a yellow stripe representing a flat plain. The tapering red and yellow areas represent tipis; at their bases, black marks representing tipi pegs bisect unpainted life symbols.

Continued from page 32

American flags, the Indians' leaders rode down to the train master with letters of introduction from various important whites.

Happy to encounter friendly Indians rather than hostile warriors, the wagon train's leaders would give them guns and ammunition as well as luxury items such as tobacco, coffee, and sugar. For these and other useful goods, the Arapahos gave the travelers safe passage through their lands.

Both the Northern Arapahos and Southern Arapahos came to have several *friendly chiefs*. These men often wore military uniforms given to them by government officials, and many learned English.

One of the Northern Arapahos' most respected friendly chiefs was known as Friday. Friday was a great hunter and fighter, but more important was his skill as a negotiator and interpreter. Friday understood white ways and spoke English because, as a child, he had been adopted by a white man named Thomas Fitzpatrick.

In 1831, Fitzpatrick was trapping along the Cimarron River in Colorado when he discovered a young Arapaho boy lost and separated from his family. Fitzpatrick named him Friday, for the day he was found, and raised him like a son. He took him to St. Louis and sent him to school. Seven years later, on a trip west with Fitzpatrick, Friday was recognized by his relatives and returned to live with his people. He became a link between whites and Arapahos.

The federal government made Thomas Fitzpatrick the Indian *agent* for the Arapahos and neighboring tribes in 1846. Indian agents worked with the Indians, carrying out U.S. government policies. In 1850, Fitzpatrick was told to organize a council between the Plains Indian tribes and the federal government. For the safety of the non-Indian population in the West, the government wanted the Indian tribes to remain in restricted areas to be decided on at the council.

The site for the meeting was on Horse Creek, in what is now Colorado. In late August of 1851, thousands of Plains Indians began arriving. Many tribes were represented: the Arapahos, Cheyennes, Sioux, Crows, Shoshones, and others. The herds of horses were so large that grass was eaten up for miles around within only a few days.

Several of the tribes were enemies who had fought many battles with one another. Nevertheless, not a single fight broke out among the 10,000 Indians present. The white officials were deeply impressed.

After two weeks of talks the Indians signed a treaty in which they agreed to stop attacks

A drawing of Denver, Colorado, in 1858. Non-Indian settlements such as Denver eventually divided the Northern and Southern Arapahos into two groups.

on United States citizens and to allow military forts to be built in their territories. They also agreed to limit warring among themselves and to live inside defined boundaries. Each tribe was assigned a particular tract of land, although they could still travel and hunt outside of these borders.

Arapaho land fell between the North Platte and the Arkansas rivers west to the foothills

of the Rocky Mountains. It was shared with
the Cheyenne Indians. In return for the con-
cessions made by the Indians, the government promised to distribute useful goods
among all the tribes once each year. Such
goods included guns, blankets, tools, cloth,
and food.

A few years after the Horse Creek treaty
was made, gold was discovered in the
Colorado Territory. Prospectors and more
whites swarmed into the area and started
settlements where the Arapahos camped
and hunted. Although whites were not permitted by the Horse Creek treaty to live in
Indian territory, the government did nothing
to stop them.

The new towns, including Denver, made it
difficult for the Northern Arapahos and Southern Arapahos to travel back and forth as they
always had for tribal councils and religious
ceremonies. They became more isolated
from each other, and by 1855 they had com-
pletely split into two groups. The Northern
Arapahos went farther north and west to
what would become Wyoming and Montana.
The Southern Arapahos moved to what is
now Colorado and Kansas, staying south of
the increasingly crowded Denver area.

The Northern Arapahos continued to hunt
on the land they shared with the Northern

Cheyenne and Sioux Indians. The Southern Arapahos, however, were overwhelmed by white settlers, who by 1860 outnumbered them 10 to 1. Game and buffalo herds were driven away, and food became scarce for the Southern Arapahos. Their situation grew even more desperate when many hunters died from cholera, smallpox, and other new diseases introduced by the whites.

Many Indians had no choice but to steal cattle from white settlers to survive. The Arapahos tried to avoid conflict with the whites, but the more warlike Cheyennes fought furiously to defend their territory.

Colorado troopers responded to the raids by attacking Cheyenne villages, killing women, children, and two friendly chiefs. The Cheyennes, along with some Arapahos, retaliated by attacking homesteaders. Most Arapahos tried to stay out of the fighting, but many whites shot any Indians they saw. Finally, the Southern Arapahos sought protection from the army.

Certain forts or military posts were suposed to offer protection to Indians weary of fighting. Sometimes army personnel went against orders and drove the Indians away. Indians who were not in the areas of protection were hunted down and killed by the troopers.

In the autumn of 1864, the army promised the Southern Arapahos and Cheyennes protection near Fort Lyon on Sand Creek. Hundreds of Indians surrendered their weapons and camped at Sand Creek. On November 29, 1864, the Colorado militia attacked them by surprise anyway. About 150 Indians were killed, most of them women and children. The massacre "was too bad to stand," according to Little Raven, leader of the remaining Southern Arapahos. They joined the Cheyennes in a fierce war against the whites.

The Northern Arapahos and their allies meeting with a U.S. peace commission in 1868.

The brutal killings committed by the army at Sand Creek shocked people in the East. Against the army's wishes, President Andrew Johnson called for peace. Although some Cheyennes continued to fight, the Southern Arapahos attended the Medicine Lodge Creek Council in 1867 and asked for a reservation in Colorado. Instead they were offered land in Kansas, where they still were not safe from the U.S. Army. Finally, in 1869 Little Raven persuaded the government to give the Southern Arapahos land in what is now Oklahoma.

The Northern Arapahos lived relatively undisturbed until 1862, when gold was discovered in Montana. Non-Indian settlements and military posts soon sprang up on their hunting grounds. The arrival of these intruders, along with the massacre of the Southern Arapahos at Sand Creek, caused the Northern Arapahos to join the Northern Cheyenne and Sioux Indians in a war against the whites, which lasted from 1865 to 1868.

After the war, the Northern Arapahos still did not have their own reservation. They did not want to move to the trouble-filled region of the Southern Arapahos. Instead, they stayed on the Sioux's reservation in the north, where at least there was still enough land for hunting. What they wanted, however, was their own reservation in Wyoming.

In 1874, a combined force of army troops and Shoshone Indians attacked a large Northern Arapaho camp. With most of their tipis, horses, and food destroyed or stolen, many

Chief Sharp Nose shaking hands with a U.S. Army captain in 1899. Sharp Nose served as head scout for the army, winning support from the government for his people.

Northern Arapahos starved or froze to death that winter.

Once again, the Arapahos would find a way to get along with their new neighbors. Led by Chief Black Coal, the Northern Arapahos survived by serving as scouts for the army, which was fighting the last Northern Cheyenne and Sioux bands that refused to settle on reservations. Scout chiefs wore army uniforms as well as feathered headdresses. They received soldiers' pay, food, and guns, and earned great respect among the tribe by sharing their earnings. But most important, serving in the army helped the Northern Arapahos gain permission to settle in Wyoming.

In 1877, President Rutherford B. Hayes agreed to speak with Northern Arapaho chiefs Black Coal, Sharp Nose, and Friday in Washington, D.C. With the army's help, they convinced the president to let them live on a Shoshone reservation in Wyoming. The Arapaho chiefs returned in triumph, wearing suits and medals given to them by President Hayes. Their wagon was filled with presents and painted black to symbolize victory. ▲

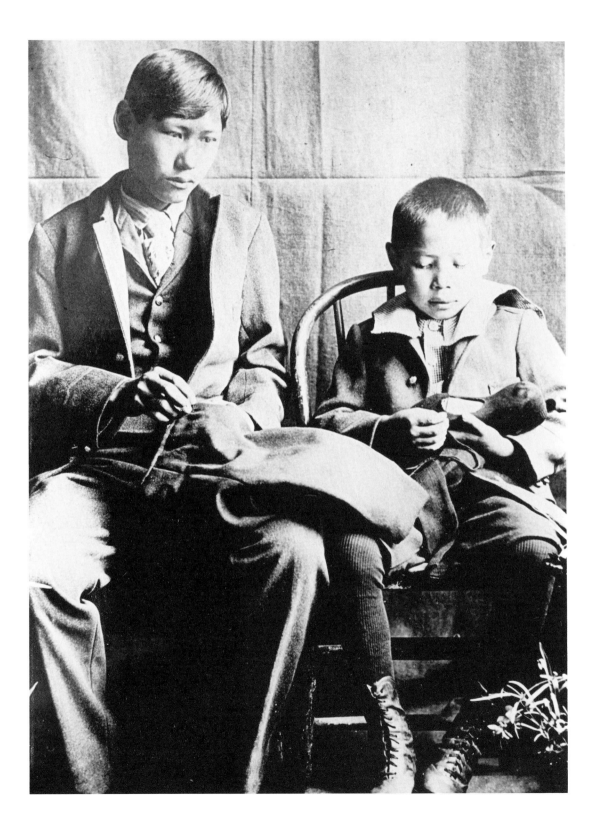

CHAPTER **4**

On Reservations

The 1870s ended with all Arapahos living on reservations. However, neither the Northern Arapahos nor the Southern Arapahos had legal ownership of the land where the government had put them. In 1871 the Southern Arapahos were sent to a reservation in Oklahoma that they shared with the Southern Cheyennes. In 1878, the Northern Arapahos settled in Wyoming on the Wind River Reservation, which they shared with the Shoshone Indians.

The Southern Arapahos' reservation was on the North Canadian River and was named the Darlington Agency, after Indian agent Brinton Darlington. At the time, the tribe's population was about 1,650. During the first years of reservation life the Southern Arapahos enjoyed an adequate food supply. A few buffalo herds migrated across nearby prairies, and the Indians hunted them in late summer and fall. Near his home at the agency, Darlington planted crops such as corn, melons, and garden vegetables, which the Arapahos harvested for their own use.

Darlington and others working at the agency were Quakers, members of a religion also known as the Society of Friends. These people were gentle with the Indians and taught them how to start farms and raise livestock by example rather than by force. The Arapahos liked the Quakers and quickly learned to plant and tend fields of crops.

Through the 1870s and 1880s many Arapaho customs, such as the lodges and naming ceremonies, continued. Whites, however, wanted Indians to become integrated into white society. They set up special schools where Indian children were separated from their parents and Indian ways were not allowed. Boys were taught to raise crops and herd cattle, and girls were taught sewing and housework.

The Arapahos did not want to send their children to these schools. Not only were they stripped of their Indian culture, but many children who went to the schools caught diseases and died. Making peace with the whites was so important to the Arapahos, however, that around 1880 Arapaho chiefs started sending their own children to one of the strictest schools, the Carlisle Indian School in Pennsylvania. As Black Coal said to federal officials, "[We] have given our children, whom we love, into their hands. We wish also to assure you by this that we never more want to go on warpath, but always live in peace."

Other Arapahos followed their leaders' example and sent their children to reservation schools. Starting at the age of nine, the

Indian men visiting the Arapaho Mercantile trading company. From left: Sumner Black Coal, Thomas Bull Chief, Yellow Plume, William Painted Red, and Old Man Scarface, an Arapaho elder.

children went to these schools for three to six years. During the summer, however, they still learned to ride ponies and listened to the ancient stories told by their grandparents.

After their schooling was complete, many young Arapahos returned to the reservation and got married. But now, a white clergyman or the Indian agent would marry the couple. Marriages were rarely arranged by the family, and men were no longer allowed to have more than one wife. Those who carried out the traditional marriage rituals were put into prison or had their food rations withheld as punishment.

The Northern Arapahos depended on food and supplies issued by the government. Unfortunately, these rations were not enough. In 1883 the Northern Arapahos received four pounds of beef per person per week. By 1889 the amount was reduced to one pound. After 1900, only the old and disabled were given anything. Even these small rations were often stolen by their white neighbors or by the government agents themselves.

The result was hunger, starvation, and death. In 1885 there were only 972 Northern Arapahos. Eight years later, their population had dropped to 823.

The Southern Arapahos' situation was better. As the buffalo dwindled away, men hunted game such as deer and wild turkey and planted corn to supplement their weekly rations. Arapaho men began to work for the Indian agency to earn money for extra food. Some became cowhands, sold wood, or hauled freight. A few worked as policemen or blacksmiths. Women took paid jobs cleaning the government school.

The Southern Arapahos cooperated with the government in the hope that they might receive special favors. They still wanted their own reservation, separate from the Cheyennes. The Cheyennes were prone to violent outbreaks with non-Indians and even went to war against the whites again in 1873–74. In contrast, the Arapahos protected the agency and escorted army troops through hostile territory. For their services they expected and often demanded gifts.

According to one agency employee, "We learned to trust the Arapaho and some of them, as they saw how much we depended upon them, became very exacting and expected many privileges. They took the liberty of entering employees' houses whenever they chose to do so, and were often annoying. They felt we owed them a great deal, and we did."

Leaders' efforts to cooperate with federal officials persuaded the government to grant

the Southern Arapahos their own reservation. In 1873 the U.S. secretary of the interior
promised to establish separate reservations
for the Southern Arapahos and the Southern
Cheyennes. Unfortunately, Congress never
ratified the agreement, and the tribes continued to share their appointed lands on the
Northern Canadian River.

The two tribes often disagreed about how
their lands should be used. In 1883, a new
agent replaced Brinton Darlington and began
leasing reservation lands to non-Indian cattle
ranchers. The income received from renting
the grazing land was to be distributed among
the tribes' members twice yearly. While the
Arapahos were agreeable to leasing, the
Cheyennes were not. Due to their protests,
President Grover Cleveland put an end to
non-Indian leasing in 1885. Cattle ranchers
continued to clamor for use of the land, however, and urged the government to abolish
the reservation altogether.

In 1887, the government dealt a crushing
blow to Indian tribes throughout the United
States by passing the General Allotment Act.
This law broke all the promises made in
treaties protecting Indian reservations. Land
that had been guaranteed to Indians forever
was broken up into small plots called *allot-*

Arapaho women in a trance during a Ghost Dance ceremony, photographed by James Mooney in 1893. While in such trances, Indians sometimes saw visions of their dead children or ancestors.

ments. Each Indian became the owner of one plot. The rest was sold to white settlers.

One purpose of the General Allotment Act was to make the Indians live like white farmers. On the dry, barren land where the Northern Arapahos lived, however, farming was almost impossible. In an agreement signed in 1904, the Northern Arapahos gave up two-thirds of their reservation and agreed to live on allotments. In return, the government gave the Indians $50 each and promised to supply them with food rations and cattle. The government also promised to provide irrigation so there would be enough water for farming.

All these promises were broken as well, and the Indians continued to go hungry. Their land was so dry that white farmers refused to buy the land the government had taken. However, the Northern Arapahos did finally gain legal title to their own land, after years of living on what was officially a Shoshone reservation.

The Southern Arapahos were hit even harder by the betrayals of the General Allotment Act. The Southern Arapahos were asked to give up about 3.5 million acres of the 4 million-acre reservation they shared with the Cheyennes. Each person would be left with a parcel of 160 acres. The Indians were horrified at this breach of trust. Their only hope for self-sufficiency was to become cattle ranchers, which would not be possible on such small allotments.

At first the tribes resisted signing the agreement, but they soon fell victim to government threats. Leaders were informed that if the document was not signed, all of their rations would be withheld. Interpreters were bribed to lie about the terms of the allotment. Signatures were even forged on the document. At last, the Arapaho leaders agreed to surrender the land, while the Cheyennes bitterly opposed the law.

One reason many Arapahos accepted the allotment policy was because they had joined a new religion called the *Ghost Dance*.

Members saw visions of their dead relatives, and they believed that the whites would disappear and the buffalo would return. As Chief Left Hand signed the agreement, he said, "I see the new land coming." A new world did come, but it was the opposite of that predicted by the followers of the Ghost Dance religion.

Homesteaders had been waiting for the reservation land to become available. When it did in April 1892, approximately 30,000 non-Indians rushed in to claim what had been Southern Arapaho and Cheyenne land for the past 20 years. Suddenly, 90 percent of the people on the former reservation were non-Indians.

Although it was not part of the agreement, government officials began setting rules designed to end the traditional Arapaho way of life. The Indian agent ordered that no encampment should include more than four families, and families were not allowed to travel to visit each other. Tribal assemblies, dances, and religious rituals were forbidden, as was the traditional Arapaho marriage. It was not even permitted for food to be shared among tribe members.

The new rules shocked the Arapahos. First their land was taken away from them, and now they were being forced to give up their freedom and traditions. This was a great blow to them after the cooperation and loyalty they had shown federal officials. Still, they chose not to fight back, unlike the Cheyennes, who again rebelled.

By the turn of the century, the Southern Arapahos suffered increasing poverty. Some of their new non-Indian neighbors felt no remorse about shooting an Indian on sight. It did not matter to them if the Indian was friendly or hostile. Property was lost to whites

who trespassed on Indian allotments and stole whatever they could, especially livestock. Homesteaders who leased Indian land often failed to pay their rent. These crimes were ignored by local authorities.

In 1902 and again in 1906, laws were passed making it easier to buy Indian lands. Many Indians were cheated out of their allotments. Scheming whites bought the land for far less than it was worth or tricked Indians into signing documents they did not understand. Shopkeepers loaned Indians money to buy food, then seized their land when they could not repay. The government's own investigation admitted that the new laws brought "joys to the grafter and confidence man, and abject poverty to the Indian." By 1920, half of the Southern Arapahos' land had been sold. By 1928, 63 percent of the original allotments were no longer owned by Arapahos.

Northern Arapaho leaders succeeded in keeping control of the lands they shared with the Shoshones, and in doing so they maintained their people's respect. But in the Oklahoma Territory there were too many whites clamoring for Indian lands, and the leaders found it impossible to stop them. Gradually, Southern Arapaho leaders lost the confidence of their people.

Northern Arapaho women working in a canning factory in 1935. The factory was built with government help under the Indian New Deal.

Despite the poverty and low morale of the tribe, traditions such as helping each other in time of need and keeping a strong relationship with the Creator held them together. Tribe members participated in traditional ceremonies as well as new ones like the Ghost Dance and the peyote ritual.

The Arapahos learned the *peyote* ritual in the 1890s from Indians to the southwest. By the 1920s, the peyote ritual was avidly practiced by younger men and women of the tribe. People who practiced the religion stayed up all night fasting, singing, and praying, after eating the peyote cactus. The plant contained a powerful drug that caused them to have visions. Like Arapahos of earlier times, they hoped for visions that would offer them guidance.

A major turning point in the Southern Arapahos' lives came in 1936. As part of President Franklin Roosevelt's Indian New Deal, the U.S. Congress passed the Oklahoma Indian Welfare Act. The remaining land of the Southern Arapahos and Cheyennes was given trust status, guaranteeing that it could not be taxed or taken away.

The Northern Arapahos and Shoshones benefited much more from the Indian New Deal. In the 1930s, the government gave

An Arapaho man and his daughter. The girl's clothing is decorated with elk's teeth, and the man is holding objects used in the peyote ritual.

back reservation land that was taken during allotment. The Indians were also given money to buy back land that had been taken and sold.

In 1947, the Wind River Indians won control over money that belonged to them from sales of their land but had been controlled until then by the secretary of the interior.

LOCATIONS OF THE ARAPAHOS TODAY

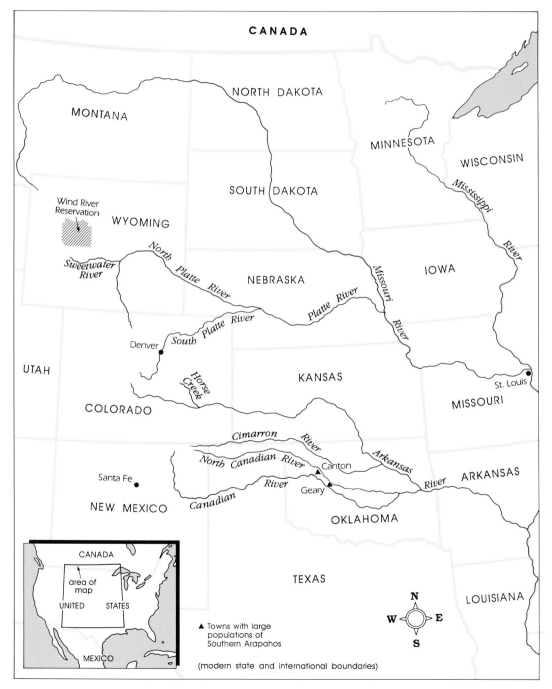

CANADA

MONTANA

NORTH DAKOTA

MINNESOTA

WISCONSIN

SOUTH DAKOTA

Wind River
Reservation

WYOMING

Mississippi

*Sweetwater
River*

North Platte River

NEBRASKA

IOWA

Platte River

Missouri River

River

UTAH

Denver

South Platte River

Horse Creek

KANSAS

St. Louis

MISSOURI

COLORADO

Cimarron River

North Canadian River

Canton

Arkansas River

ARKANSAS

Santa Fe

River

Geary

NEW MEXICO

Canadian

OKLAHOMA

CANADA

area of
map

UNITED   STATES

TEXAS

LOUISIANA

N
W   E
S

MEXICO

▲ Towns with large
populations of
Southern Arapahos

(modern state and international boundaries)

Claiming the Indians would not spend these funds wisely, the government had been using the Indians' own money to build agency buildings and pay agency staff. With the new income, the Northern Arapahos built dozens of new homes and installed electricity for the whole community. In 1961, the Northern and Southern Arapahos, together with the Cheyennes, won a multimillion-dollar settlement from the government over treaty violations.

The Southern Arapahos, however, never got their land back. Because there was no way to make a living on what little land they had left, many were driven to urban areas to seek employment. In 1951, only one-third of the Southern Arapahos still owned even a small piece of their families' original allotments.

Those in the towns and cities often returned to the countryside for ceremonies and dances. But after 1930, the Southern Arapahos had to travel to Wyoming for the Offerings Lodge, their most important ceremony. Without a shared reservation, their community and traditions were disintegrating. ▲

*Jimmy Oldman and grand-
son Patrick Atencio at a
school powwow on the
Wind River Reservation.*

CHAPTER 5

Arapahos Today

In the 1960s, presidents John Kennedy and Lyndon Johnson introduced new government programs called the New Frontier and the Great Society. These programs helped minority groups by offering them better education, housing, and job training.

Indian communities benefited greatly from these programs. On many Indian lands and in urban Indian communities, housing projects were funded and water supplies and sanitation facilities were improved. Many preschool children were enrolled in the Head Start program. Older Indian children learned about their history and traditions in school.

Whenever possible, Indians were given control over programs affecting them. As part of President Johnson's War on Poverty, Indian business councils were paid by the federal government to run the programs within their communities. Funding for such programs continued through the 1970s.

The social programs of the 1960s and 1970s came to a halt under President Ronald Reagan. In the 1980s, budget cuts put an end to many government-funded jobs and reduced medical and social services for the needy. The situation was made worse by a worldwide decline in oil prices. This affected both the Wind River Arapahos and Oklahoma Arapahos, who receive royalties from oil wells on their land.

Today, most Southern Arapahos live in tribal housing projects in Geary, Oklahoma, or in private homes in Canton, Oklahoma. Only a few live on inherited allotments. Out of the original half a million acres of allotments, only 15 percent are still owned by Southern Arapahos. Some elders who held on to parts of their families' allotments lease their land to oil and gas companies.

The schools and other agency buildings at the Darlington Agency closed between the years of 1920 and 1970, and the grounds and surrounding lands were given back to the Southern Arapahos and the Southern Cheyennes. Today this land, totaling 10,000 acres, is shared by the tribes. It is leased for farming and grazing. These leases bring the tribes about $130,000 a year. The money is used to support programs to assist the needy and to cover operating expenses of the tribal government. Oil and gas royalties provide a second income from the communal land. This money is given out in small per-person payments every year.

Oklahoma Arapahos are poor, with most living below the poverty level. In recent years, their unemployment rate has been between 40 percent and 70 percent. The Arapahos also have to contend with discrimination by non-Indians when looking for work. Most families are subsidized by the federal government, receiving Social Security or military pensions.

Together with the Southern Cheyennes, the Southern Arapahos continue to elect a business council. Members supervise federally funded programs and represent the tribe in their dealings with oil and gas companies, cattle ranchers, and all levels of the government. In recent years, they have worked to establish three tribally owned businesses, including a bingo parlor.

Elders of Southern Arapaho society are still treated with great respect. But because Oklahoma is no longer a center for Arapaho religious ritual, much of the elders' former role as a link between the people and the Creator has been lost.

Unlike the Northern Arapaho children, who go to special reservation schools, the Southern Arapahos attend regular public schools. Some young men and women earn college degrees and work as managers on tribal projects, but many have to leave their

Polly C'Bearing of the Wyoming Indian High School Lady Chiefs.

communities to seek employment in distant cities.

Because they have no shared reservation, benefit dances serve as the center of Southern Arapaho social life. Held every weekend in Geary or Canton, Oklahoma, the dances function as fundraisers for many community causes such as aiding the needy and paying for summer gatherings called powwows.

The Geary Arapahos hold a powwow every July, and the Canton Arapahos sponsor one in August. Both the Arapahos and Cheyennes come together for a larger powwow in September. At powwows, families perform their traditional dances and songs; share food, crafts, and folklore; and honor their leaders and elders.

The peyote ritual is still widely practiced, and once a year many Southern Arapahos travel to the Wind River Reservation in Wyoming to join the Northern Arapahos for the Offerings Lodge.

Today, the Northern Arapaho population is about 4,000. Most Northern Arapahos still live on their family allotments in private homes. Their reservation is 70 miles by 50 miles of open land bordered at either end by small towns, where the Indians go to shop. Otherwise, they have few connections with the non-Indian communities.

Northern Arapaho children are raised in large extended families. Parents, aunts, uncles, and grandparents act as one giant family, so every child is raised with many parents and grandparents. Cousins are raised as brothers and sisters. As they grow up, children even move from one relative's house to another's. They are taught to be unselfish, repress their anger, and respect their elders.

Public schools on the Wind River Reservation teach the children Arapaho history, traditions, language, and handicrafts, as well as the subjects taught in non-Indian schools. Sports are enjoyed by all age groups. Teenagers take pride in their high school teams, which often defeat neighboring non-Indian schools. Like the Southern Arapahos, the Wind River group has social clubs and benefit dances which raise money and bring people together.

After high school, many youths attend college, enlist in the armed services, or take jobs on the reservation. Today, more couples are marrying in their teens, before they are self-supporting. Although they may have their own homes in a tribal housing project, they continue to spend much time with their extended families. Some find work on the reservation on projects funded by the federal

Wyoming Indian High School students carry a banner on American Indian Day. The banner reads, Going Back To Tradition: Wisdom, Bravery, Respect, Generosity.

government. But there are few of these jobs, and the unemployment rate is well over 50 percent. Those who have work help to support relatives without jobs.

Oil and gas royalties provide the Northern Arapahos with a stable source of income. Eighty-five percent of this money is divided into equal shares and paid directly to each member of the tribe. The rest is administered by a business council.

The six-member business council works with the Shoshone council to manage the reservation's resources. They run a cattle ranch the tribe has owned since 1940, and other businesses such as a gas station and two grocery stores. The council decides who can lease tribal lands, giving preference to Indians, and buys land from families wishing to sell their allotments. Seventy-eight percent of the 2 ½-million-acre reservation is tribally owned, and most of the rest is owned by individual Arapahos.

Although the business council is the acting leadership of the Arapahos, the entire tribe has to agree on major decisions. The opinions of elders continue to have a great deal of influence within the tribe.

A group of elderly men and women supervises all sacred ceremonies at Wind River. One leader cares for the Sacred Pipe. This object represents the supernatural power available to the Arapahos if they live in harmony with one another and fulfill their ritual responsibilities.

Of all rituals and ceremonies, the Offerings Lodge continues to be the most important. For seven days in July, both the Northern and Southern tribes camp together at Wind River, where participants fulfill their sacred vows. Everyone concentrates on cooperation and harmony during these days. Food is prepared by all families and shared throughout the camp as an affirmation of unity.

In the lodge, the story of the duck and the turtle and the creation of the world is acted out. People pray, fast, and offer sacrifices as a way of renewing their relationship to the Creator.

Today, the Arapahos continue to struggle for what they believe is theirs, taking the government to task when necessary. Although some live in the non-Indian world, all share a cultural identity that lends them strength and makes them feel proud. The Northern and Southern Arapahos have been separated by hundreds of miles of prairie and different experiences over the last hundred years. But they continue to share a language, a rich history and tradition, and a strong faith in the great mystery above. ▲

CHRONOLOGY

1803   United States buys the Louisiana Purchase, a large tract of land that includes the Arapahos' territory

1851   At the Horse Creek Council, the U.S. government convinces Plains Indians to live within defined boundaries

Nov. 29, 1864   Colorado Militia slaughters a camp of Southern Arapahos and Cheyennes at the Sand Creek massacre, after the Indians had been promised protection and had surrendered their weapons

1871   Southern Arapahos move onto a reservation in Oklahoma with the Southern Cheyennes

1874   Army troops and Shoshone Indians attack Northern Arapahos, leaving them without tipis or food for the winter

1878   Northern Arapahos settle on Wind River Reservation in Wyoming with the Shoshones

1887   U.S. Congress passes General Allotment Act, which calls for the division of reservation lands into individual plots called allotments

Apr. 19, 1892   Reservation of Southern Arapahos and Cheyennes is opened to white settlers

1904   Wind River Reservation is allotted; Northern Arapahos and Shoshones lose two-thirds of their land

1930   The last Offerings Lodge ceremony in Oklahoma is held

1930s   President Franklin D. Roosevelt's Indian New Deal ends allotment; Northern Arapahos regain lost reservation land

1961   Arapahos and Cheyennes win multimillion dollar settlement from the U.S. government

GLOSSARY

agent   an employee of the U.S. government responsible for conducting official business with an Indian tribe

allotment   a policy of the U.S. government to divide Indian reservations into small, privately owned plots of land; also, one of these plots

buffalo chips   dried buffalo droppings, which the Arapahos burned as fuel

friendly chief   an Indian chief who greeted non-Indian travelers and escorted them through dangerous territory in exchange for gifts

Ghost Dance   an Indian religion popular in the late 1800s that promised whites would disappear and the buffalo would return

lodge   a sacred society that Arapaho men joined to gain spiritual power, earn respect, and perform service to the community

Offerings Lodge   a ceremony in which participants danced without rest for days until they had visions; also called the Sacrifice Lodge or the Sun Dance

peyote   a cactus used in the peyote ritual; parts of the cactus contain a powerful drug that can help the user have visions

reservation   an area of land set aside by the U.S. government for Indian use

tipi   a portable, cone-shaped house made out of wooden poles covered with sewn buffalo hides

INDEX

INDEX

ABOUT THE AUTHOR

VICKI HALUSKA is a writer living in New York City.

PICTURE CREDITS